IN THE
GARDEN

D1354004

Sunflower
Flowers: July–September. This unmistakable, daisy-like flower will grow to a height of up to 3 metres. It prefers dryish soil and, as its name suggests, loves a sunny position in the garden.
I-Spy for **15**

Tulip
Flowers: April–May. The tulip is a spring flower. It originates from Turkey and was brought to Europe in the mid-sixteenth century. Look out for lots of different varieties, many of which are cultivated in Holland. Colours range from red to pink to white and yellow, with various combinations between.
I-Spy for **15**

Echinacea
Flowers: July–October. You should be able to I-Spy this plant in a sunny border. Its daisy-like head has a central cone surrounded by petals that can vary in colour from a rich purple to white.
I-Spy for **10**

Roses

Flowers: June–July. Grown for their fragrance and beautiful flowers, you are likely to find roses in most gardens. Though thought of as the 'classic' English flower, cultivated roses were developed from the Eurasian sweetbriar. Roses were first reared in monasteries and can either form a bush or appear as a climber.
I-Spy 5 for each of a climber, rambler, floribunda (flowers in large sprays), and hybrid tea (large-bloomed and often sweetly scented)

Aster

Flowers: August–September. We know some varieties of aster as Michaelmas daisies – so named because they are in flower at the time of the Michaelmas festival on 29 September. They grow in borders and in rock gardens. The flowers are usually pink or purple in colour.
I-Spy for 15

Hosta

Flowers: July–August. Hostas are found mostly in damp, shady positions in the garden. They are grown for their striking foliage and trumpet-like flowers. See if you can find varieties with 'bluish' and variegated leaves (white streaks).
I-Spy for 15

Fern
There are over 10,000 different varieties of fern, most of which are found in the tropics. They like humid, shady conditions and are often found in wooded areas. This one is the shuttlecock fern.

I-Spy 15 for the shuttlecock fern and 15 for each of 3 other kinds

Yucca
Flowers: July–August. The yucca is a palm-like shrub with striking, sword-shaped leaves. It likes warm climates, so you are more likely to find it in the southern counties of England. Smaller examples make successful houseplants.
I-Spy for 25

Sempervivum
Flowers: July. Often found in the rockery, the sempervivum, or houseleek, is one of the succulent group of plants, with its fleshy leaves forming a neat rosette.
I-Spy for 15

The mixed border

Typically consisting of trees, shrubs, and flowers, the mixed border provides a home for a great variety of different plants. But, because of the trend towards smaller gardens and considering the amount of work required to keep them in trim, they are becoming harder to I-Spy nowadays.

I-Spy 15 for a mixed border,
5 for each of 6 different flowers you can name in it

Other borders

Look out, too, for other types of border in the garden – each might be devoted to a particular colour theme or type of plant, for example. This one is made up entirely of Michaelmas daisies.

I-Spy 20 for a Michaelmas daisy border, 10 each for 2 others

5

Garden herbs

Herbs were traditionally grown for use in the kitchen. Today, they make interesting plants, each with its own peculiar history. In this picture (*from left*) is the tall Welsh onion, chives, monarda just behind (the leaves of which are used in Earl Grey tea when the plant is better known as berga-mot), tarragon behind that, the yellowish golden marjoram in the front, and silver-leafed sage at front right.

I-Spy **15** *for each of 4 different kinds*

Water-lily

Flowers: February–March. Not all plants grow on land. The lily is suspended on the surface of the water and will bloom in daytime. Water-lilies help to keep the water clear because their leaves provide shade and prevent the growth of algae.

I-Spy for **20**

Climbers

Some plants prefer to go upwards rather than outwards. Such examples offer an attractive display against a wall or fence. This is clematis. Other popular climbing plants include roses, honeysuckle, ivy, and the Virginia creeper with its leaves that turn a striking red colour in autumn.

I-Spy **10** *for each of four different kinds other than roses*

Heathers

Flowers: All year round. Heaths and heathers provide ornamental value all-year-round as well as good ground cover. Natives of peaty, acid soils, they can, in fact, be grown under a variety of conditions.
I-Spy for **15**

Grasses

Growing season: All year round. Grasses add colour and architectural form to a garden. They love sunny, well-drained positions and can either be grouped together or placed among other plants for maximum contrast.
I-Spy **5** *for lawn grass,* **15** *for another kind*

Weeds

Every garden has weeds, much to the annoyance of the gardener! But some are quite attractive and could easily be mistaken for more welcome additions to the garden. Some resemble thistles, some form a suffocating ground cover, and some twine themselves around other plants or are sticky. How many different types of weed can you spot?
I-Spy **5** *for each of 4 different weeds*

Rhododendron

The rhododendron gets its name from the Greek words *rhodon* (meaning 'rose') and *dendron* ('tree'). Different kinds grow wild throughout the northern hemisphere but they are especially abundant in the Himalayas. They do best in woodland where there is shade, shelter from wind, and rich soil. They can grow to a height of 20 metres. They produce flowers in a great variety of colours from early spring until the end of summer.

I-Spy 15 for each of 4 different colour varieties

Marigold

Flowers: June–October. Both the French and the African varieties of this pretty yellow flower originate from Mexico. Their foliage produces a strong smell when crushed.

I-Spy for 10

Geranium

Flowers: Throughout the summer. Though often referred to as a geranium, the real name of this flower is pelargonium. It is perhaps one of our most common plants. Geraniums make a colourful display in window boxes and hanging baskets, and they also live indoors as houseplants during the winter. Look out for the fancy-leaf varieties with their interesting and unusual leaf patterns.

I-Spy for 5

Lupins

The stately spires of the lupin carry pea-like flowers in June and July in a variety of spectacular colours. It has become one of the most popular flowers in the garden.

I-Spy for **5**

Snowdrops

The tiny white flowers of the snowdrop herald the start of a new year in the garden, and appear from January through until March.

I-Spy for **15**

Crocus

It is, perhaps, just a coincidence that the flowering season of the crocus falls just after the snowdrop and just before the tulip – thus providing a continuous display of colour throughout spring. It has either purple or yellow flowers, or a combination of the two.

I-Spy for **15**

Narcissus
If the central cup of the Narcissus is longer than the petals, then it is called by its common name, daffodil. As the leek is a national plant of Wales, the daffodil is that country's national flower. Its pretty yellow flowers herald the start of spring.
I-Spy for 5

Chrysanthemum
There are hundreds of different varieties of chrysanthemum, and their flowers are either flat and daisy-like or shaggy and rounded like this example. They can also be grown indoors and, under the right conditions in the greenhouse, can be made to flower all year round.
I-Spy for 10

Delphinium
The towering spires of the delphinium, in blue, purple, and white, are easily recognizable in the garden. They enjoy fertile, well-drained soil, and, if cut back after their main flowering season in June–July, will produce a final burst of colour in autumn.
I-Spy for 10

Dahlia

Originating from Mexico, the dahlia provides an ideal plant for the border. It grows to about knee height, and produces flowers from July to November in a wide variety of colours.

*I-Spy **10** for each of single, double, cactus, and pompon varieties.*

Gladiolus

Flowers: July–September. The spectacular display of the gladioli can be seen in many gardens, and there is a wide variety of different types and colours. The flowers of the miniatures, for instance, are less than 10 millimetres across while the giants can be 14 centimetres across.

*I-Spy for **10***

The summerhouse

This is often the retreat of gardeners while enjoying a well-earned rest from their labours. A summerhouse has a large window area to allow as much sunlight as possible to reach the interior. Some older, more elaborate summerhouses can even be turned to follow the sun.

I-Spy for **15**

The conservatory

Thought of as a 'garden room', the conservatory forms a link between the house and the garden. Its airiness and humidity make it an ideal place to relax among the plants during the colder seasons.

I-Spy for **5**

Gazebo

Loosely, its Latin meaning, 'I will gaze', provides a clue to its original purpose. Positioned on a raised terrace, the gazebo offers a sheltered place from which to view the garden.

I-Spy for **20**

Greenhouse

By providing shelter, the greenhouse speeds up the growing rate of plants and protects the less resilient plants against cold weather. Look out for whitewashed glass in summer – this is used to protect plants from being scorched by bright sunshine.
I-Spy for 15

Garden shed

No garden would be complete without the garden shed. It is used mainly for storing garden tools, lawnmowers, and seed, etc.
I-Spy for 5

Arbour

Originally, garden arbours were decorative structures used for festivals and pageants. Today, they are commonly used to grow climbers such as roses, clematis, and honeysuckle.
I-Spy for 15

Pergola

The pergola is used to add height and perspective to the garden. Typically, it is made of wood, but see if you can spot some more grandiose examples incorporating brick and stone.
I-Spy for 15

General implements

Four of the most common tools used by gardeners – (*at the back*) a fork and a spade for digging and turning over the soil; (*at the front*) a Dutch hoe for weeding and a rake for breaking up the soil. These versions are specially for children, so they are smaller than usual.

I-Spy 50 for all 4

Lawn rake

Gardens can look uncared-for when trees lose their leaves in autumn. One of the easiest ways of tidying up the lawn is with a lawn rake. If leaves are left, they could cause turf disease and reduce the amount of evaporation from the lawn.

I-Spy for 10

Pruning tools

A different tool for different jobs: from the pruning knife used to cut the stems of shoots, secateurs used to cut larger stems, to the pruning saw that makes short work of small branches.

I-Spy 10 for each of 3 different pruning tools

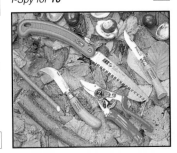

Compost shredder and lawn roller

The compost shredder is the environmentally friendly way of ridding the garden of unwanted waste. The result of the shredding is then used as compost. The lawn roller in the background, used to create the perfect lawn, is quite a rare sight these days. It has been replaced by easier-to-use plastic versions.

I-Spy 20 for each

Wheelbarrow

This is a rarely seen example made from wood. More often, wheel-barrows are manufactured from galvanized steel or plastic.

I-Spy 50 for a wooden wheelbarrow, 10 for one made of metal or plastic

Plant labels

Labels are used in the garden to help the visitor identify different plant varieties – often in Latin. They are also used by gardeners to help them remember what they have planted where! The ones in this picture are made from metal. Look out, too, for ceramic plant labels and, more commonly, ones made from plastic.

I-Spy 25 for metal labels like these, 10 for any other

Old tools

Just some examples of gardening tools from yesteryear. Pictured are metal watering cans, wooden seed trays, some terracotta pots, a fork, and a wooden trug used for collecting garden produce.

I-Spy 25 for any one of these

Special tools

These are all long-handled tools for people who have difficulty bending down or for gardeners in wheel-chairs.

I-Spy for 50

Lawn mowers

These are all modern versions of the lawn mower. See if you can spot the differences between the rotary mowers in the foreground and the more traditional cylinder mowers above them at the back. Keep an eye out, too, for ride-on mowers which are usually found in larger gardens.

I-Spy 20 for an old-fashioned mower, 10 for a modern one

Peas

These are among the most delicious garden vegetables – but beware, birds and mice like to eat them, too, so they are best protected by netting or by wire pea-guards. Most peas have green pods (though there is a purple-podded variety). Early crops will be ready at the end of May or early June, while the main harvest will be from mid-June onwards.

I-Spy for 15
Double for mangetout or sugar-snap peas which have edible pods

Lettuces

Most salads would be incomplete without lettuce, which can be grown in greenhouses early or late in the season or in the garden in summer. Look out for well-known varieties such as Webb's Wonderful, Little Gem, and Tom Thumb.

I-Spy 10 for each of 3 different kinds of lettuce

Cabbages

Cabbages can be picked from the garden throughout the year. Spring cabbages, ready in April or May, are usually small and are often started under a cold frame or cloche to protect them from cold weather. Summer and autumn cabbages are ready from the end of June to September or October, and winter varieties mature from October to January.

I-Spy for 15
Double for red cabbage

Broccoli

Between February and May, look out for two types – purple- and white-sprouting broccolis. The purple varieties are hardier and more prolific but both attract pests such as slugs and pigeons.

I-Spy for 20

Beetroot

These come in many shapes – pointed (oval), round, flat, and long rooted. They can be pulled any time between late spring and autumn and, for eating, they are sometimes pickled in vinegar.

I-Spy for 15

Potato

This is our most popular vegetable and one of the most versatile – potatoes can be baked, mashed, boiled or baked, or chopped into chips and fried. Early varieties, lifted in June or July, are known as new potatoes, while the main crop is ready in September. Popular varieties include Maris Piper, Majestic, Golden Wonder, and Pentland Crown.

I-Spy 10 each for a red and white variety

18

Radishes

Salad radishes are among the easiest vegetables for children to grow. But there are other, more unusual varieties, too, including those with small yellow roots, giant Japanese types, and one which is grown for its leaves rather than its roots. Summer varieties crop between May and August while winter ones are lifted from late October.

I-Spy 10 for salad radishes, 25 for any other kind

Cauliflower

Cauliflowers are difficult to grow because they need a lot of rain and good soil. Depending on the variety, they can be harvested between early spring and November although, on the south coast of England and in Wales, winter cauli-flowers are cut between December and March.

I-Spy for 15

Broad beans

This vegetable has been cultivated for centuries and is one of the easiest of all to grow. Most people eat the large, greeny white beans found inside the pods but the leaf tips can also be cooked. Picking usually takes place between May and August. Beware of letting the pods get too big for then the beans will be tough.

I-Spy for 10

Asparagus

Crops: April–June. Asparagus is a member of the fern family and is produced for its young shoots or 'spears'. Despite being expensive to buy in the shops, it will grow for twenty years or more and makes an attractive addition to the garden.

I-Spy for 50

Sweet peppers

Crops: August–September. Sweet peppers belong to the same family as tomatoes and potatoes. If left on the plant, they will turn from green to red. They need high temperatures and humidity to grow and so will often be found in the greenhouse or in a cloche.

I-Spy for 25

French beans

Crops: July–October. Also known as kidney beans, they are grown either for their pods, which are eaten when young, or for their shelled beans when mature. Look out too for the yellow wax-pod varieties.

I-Spy for 15 and I-Spy 10 for runner or string beans

Onions

Crops: July–September. This is the common onion that you will find in most vegetable plots. But there are other less common varieties to look out for. One is the 'Egyptian' or 'tree onion' which produces aerial bulbs as it climbs. There are also red-skinned types with reddish pigment in the outer layers.

I-Spy for **10, 10** *for spring onion,* **25** *for tree onion*

Tomatoes

Crops: July–October. Originally from South America, the tomato is easy to grow and comes in a number of different shapes, colours, and sizes. The largest variety is the 'beefsteak' which can grow to the size of a small football; the smallest include the 'cherry' tomato which is about 2.5 centimetres in diameter. There are also pear-shaped tomatoes, ones with stripes, and others that are pink, orange, and yellow. How many different ones can you spot?

I-Spy for **5, 25** *for other colours*

Rhubarb

Classed as a vegetable, and not a fruit, because of its delicately flavoured, reddish-pink leaf stalks, the rhubarb has enormous leaves which contain oxalic acid and are therefore poisonous. It is in season from March to July but using a forcer like this one allows crops to be harvested in January and February.
I-Spy for **10**

Ornamental cabbage

Fruits: March–May. A cabbage with a difference that will add colour to any vegetable plot. But you can't eat it, more's the pity!
I-Spy for **25**

Marrows and courgettes

Crops: July–October. Basically, courgettes are immature marrows grown from varieties that have tender skins for eating. See if you can spot striped and round forms of courgettes and ones with yellow skins.
I-Spy for **15**

Gunnera

Flowers: July–September. This spectacular plant with enormous leaves, spiky stems, and unusual cone-like flowers is most likely to be found at the side of a pond or in damp, shady positions.
I-Spy for **50**

Venus flytrap

The Venus flytrap is perhaps one of the most remarkable of all the carnivorous plants that entice and trap insects for food. It is a bog plant, native of South Carolina in the United States. You might just find one in a garden centre or botanical garden. How many other carnivorous plants can you name?

I-Spy for **50**

Chinese lantern

Flowers: June–August. In autumn the membrane that surrounds the fruit inflates to create this unusual bright-red lantern. The dried fruits are often used for winter decorations.
I-Spy for **25**

Blue poppy
Flowers: June–July. Otherwise known as the Himalayan poppy, this variety makes an unusual contrast to its common red cousin. It can sometimes be seen growing in peaty, acid soils.
*I-Spy for **50***

Eryngium
Flowers: June–August. This spiky plant has dramatic, thistle-like leaves with a bluish tinge, and, as its common name, sea holly, would suggest, it is happiest in the dry, sandy soil of its native seaside home.
*I-Spy for **20***

24

Bonsai

The art of bonsai lies in the pruning of top growth and roots to produce a specimen identical to a tree in every respect except for its miniature size. Originally perfected by the Japanese, good examples fetch large sums of money today.
I-Spy for **25**

Fritillaria

Flowers: April–May. This unusual plant has a long stem and peculiar bell-like flowers topped with a crown of narrow leaves – giving rise to its rather stately variety name, 'Crown Imperial'. Its flowers are either red or yellow.
I-Spy for **25**

Cacti

Usually found in the desert, the cactus can sometimes be seen in the garden. Its spiky form serves to retain water in times of drought and protects it from preying animals. In contrast to its prickly nature, it often produces beautiful and delicate flowers.
I-Spy for **20**

Walls

Brick is one of the best materials to use for boundaries – the result is strong and attractive, heights can vary, and plants can be grown up the sides.

*I-Spy for **5** and I-Spy **50** for a 'wavy wall'*

Metal railings

Railings like these have been popular for centuries. The beauty of them is that they don't interfere with the views on either side. One drawback is that they offer no protection against strong winds.

*I-Spy for **5***

Railings

Wrought iron fences like these, with curled sections, can look extremely grand. Unfortunately, they must be painted regularly to prevent them becoming rusty.

*I-Spy for **10***

Fence in disguise
A wrought iron fence in disguise. This is actually made from wood though you can't tell just from looking at it. To find out, you would have to touch it.
I-Spy for 20

Board fencing
A simple style of fence, made from wooden boards placed horizontally. This is ideal for keeping out wildlife, particularly from vegetable plots.
I-Spy for 15

Hedges
For generations, hedges have been used as garden boundaries. Privet hedges, like this one, form a dense barrier, but have to be trimmed regularly. Beech, box, and yew are also grown as hedges. Some gardeners clip theirs into unusual shapes such as trains, people, or nursery rhyme characters. This practice is called topiary.
I-Spy 10 for each of 4 different kinds of hedge

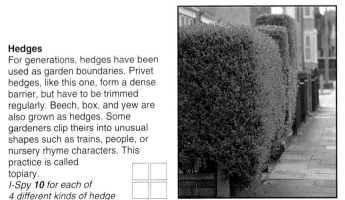

Classical wall

The grand gardens of big country houses probably provided inspiration for this stone-effect wall. Here it is used to separate different areas of the same garden.

I-Spy for **25**

Stone wall

Local stone was often a good source of material for walls, as shown here. It would be quarried not far away so that the cost of transport would not be too high.

I-Spy for **15**

Garden gnome
This little chap, and his friends, have been popular garden ornaments for many years. One of the very first garden gnomes can be found in the nineteenth-century rock garden at Lamport Hall in Northamptonshire. It was insured for one million pounds when it appeared at the Chelsea Flower Show!
I-Spy for 20

Scarecrow
For centuries, fearsome-looking models like this have been used to frighten crows, pigeons, and other pests from young crops such as beans and peas. These days, scarecrows are also used as garden ornaments.
I-Spy for 50

Windvane
Look at the roofs of garden buildings and you could well find a revolving windvane like this. Its main use is to show from which direction the wind is blowing but they come in some very decorative and imaginative designs.
I-Spy for 20

GARDEN FEATURES

Bird boxes
Birds, such as blue tits, wrens, and owls, are welcome visitors to gardens. To encourage their presence, remember to put out bird seed and scraps of food, particularly in bad weather, and place a bird box like this in a quiet place away from prowling animals.
I-Spy for 10

Bird table
A conventional bird table, sheltering birds and food from rain. This version, with a thatched roof, has been made to look like an old-fashioned cottage.
I-Spy for 10

Bird bath
Birds like water to drink and to bathe in, so a bird bath is a good idea for any gardener who wants to attract wildlife to the garden.
I-Spy for 10

Dovecote

Dovecotes are, quite literally, houses for doves, attractive white members of the pigeon family. Dovecotes are usually made from wood and placed high off the ground, out of the reach of predators. Some dovecotes, particularly on larger houses, can be quite grand and ornamental.
I-Spy for 20

Sundials

In the days before clocks were common, sundials like this were useful for telling the time – depending on where the shadow of the arm (called a gnomon) fell, people could work out the hour. These days, sundials are usually ornamental although, if they have been correctly positioned, they can still be used to tell the time.
I-Spy for 25

Fountain

This sculpture, showing a boy and girl in Victorian costume, is also a fountain – water trickles on to the pebbles at the base.

I-Spy for 15

Sandpit

Most children would agree that no garden is complete without a sandpit. This version fits neatly into the patio area and can be covered with the lid when not in use.

I-Spy for 15

Bench

Garden seats can be found in a wide variety of shapes and materials. This rustic-looking version also includes a storage cupboard, useful for tools and other implements.

I-Spy for 5

Modern statue

Sculptures, such as this sheep, are popular garden ornaments. Unlike their traditional counterparts, they are made from cast concrete, a contemporary material.

I-Spy for 15

Classical statue

Large, formal gardens often contain classically inspired statues such as this imposing stone eagle. Where did you find your classical statue?

_____

I-Spy for 15

Pond

Ponds, whether they are formal or natural like this one, form attractive features in a garden. This example has been carefully cultivated to attract as much wildlife as possible.

I-Spy for 10

Vegetable garden

Rows of onions, beans, parsley and other crops can be found in the traditional vegetable or kitchen garden. Here, a glass cloche is also used to protect vulnerable lettuces from cold weather and pests. Years ago, most householders grew as many sources of food as possible. These days, it is easy to buy fruit and vegetables from supermarkets, regardless of the season.

I-Spy for **10**
Double for a vegetable garden with cloches

Rock garden

This is an ideal setting for small, slow-growing plants that need free-draining soil. As far as possible, rock gardens duplicate the natural habitat of alpine plants – sloping, well-drained, gritty soil with rocky outcrops. Here, carpets of sedum and saxifrage flourish.

I-Spy for **20**

Lawned garden

A classic, English image – a large lawned area is broken up by a crescent-shaped flower border. In large country houses such as this, a small army of gardeners would once have tended the grounds. These days there is likely to be just one or two.

I-Spy for **5** for a lawned garden and I-Spy **5** for each of six different flowers you can name

Oriental garden
Japanese-style gardens take inspiration from hills, lakes, and islands, and feature thick plantings of dwarf trees and shrubs, symbolic groups of shaped stones, and gravel paths leading to stone lanterns. Where did you find your Japanese garden?

I-Spy for **50**

Mediterranean garden
In a hot, Mediterranean climate, whitewashed walls, pantiled roofs, shaded terraces, and lush green borders provide a cool, relaxing effect. Where did you find your Mediterranean garden?

I-Spy for **50**

35

Cottage garden

A traditional cottage garden had flowers, shrubs, herbs, and vegetables crowded into a small area. This example includes a twig 'wigwam' to support trailing beans. As much room as possible is taken up with growing plants, once the householder's main source of food.

I-Spy 15 for a cottage garden and I-Spy 5 for each of 5 different plants you can name

Parterres

Unlike many garden features, these are best viewed from above. They are intricate designs of low, interlacing box hedge enclosing contrasting coloured plants. This is part of the world-famous garden at Villandry, in France, but the tradition was also popular in many British parks.

I-Spy for 50

Water garden

Here is a natural-looking water garden which has actually been planned very carefully to blend into its surroundings. The slope provides an ideal opportunity for small waterfalls.

I-Spy for 15

Slabs

Coloured paving slabs can form an attractive, patterned path as shown here. The result is a distinctive walkway bordered by hedges of lavender.
I-Spy for 10

Pebble patterns

Pebbles laid in a mosaic style provide an unusual, yet eye-catching, display for a terrace or patio. These have been painted to create an even more dynamic effect.
I-Spy for 50

Slate

Here slate pieces form a 'crazy-paving' area beneath a swing. Crazy-paving looks very haphazard but in reality has to be worked out carefully. Where did you find your crazy-paving?

_____

_____

I-Spy for 15

Bricks
Old blue bricks give a cottage feel to this walled vegetable garden. It looks as though the path has been widened at some point – note the different styles of brick.
I-Spy for **10**

Stone slabs
Old stone slabs provide an attractive base for this quiet corner. Once weathered, they blend well with the ironstone wall and inset sculptures.
I-Spy for **15**

Gravel
A low box hedge separates the rose border from the gravel path. On the other side of the walkway is a conifer tree nursery.
I-Spy for **5**

Fox

Foxes are becoming increasingly common in urban, as well as rural, areas and will often scavenge from dustbins. Foxes may damage lawns – they rip up grass to feed on chafer larvae.

I-Spy for 25

Hedgehog

Known as the gardener's friend, hedgehogs are useful because they feed on many ground-dwelling pests such as slugs. If you find a hedgehog in your garden, leave piles of dead leaves as a hibernation site and always check before setting bonfires alight – hedgehogs have a habit of curling up inside them. Never feed hedgehogs with bread and milk – tinned pet food is better.

I-Spy for 25

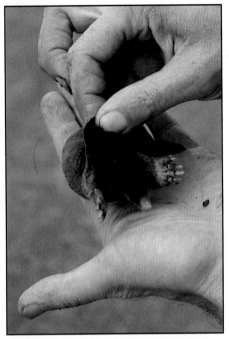

Mole

You are more likely to see molehills (small mounds of earth) than moles, the small brown, furry creatures that make them. They live underground for most of their lives and excavate tunnels with their front legs.
I-Spy 10 for a molehill, 50 if you actually I-Spy a mole!

Earthworm

Worms usually have a good effect on soil – they increase its fertility and drainage. They live on dead and dying plants, and can usually be found in the top 50 centimetres of the soil. There may be up to 500 worms in every square metre of grass.
I-Spy for 10

Pears

Pears are closely related to apples, but pear trees are usually found growing in the southern counties of Britain. Trees flower in spring and bear fruit from late August through to October.
I-Spy for 25

Cherries

Introduced into Britain by the Romans, cherries can be eaten straight from the tree or the sour ones can be cooked, depending on variety. They range in colour from pale yellow to almost black. Most fruit is ripe for picking in July.
I-Spy for 20

Gooseberries

Gooseberry bushes have sharp thorns and they are sometimes found growing wild. They fruit in July and will survive in the garden with very little attention.
I-Spy for 20

Raspberries

Raspberries bear fruit in summer or autumn depending on variety. The plants are usually supported by canes or are trained to grow against a wall. They thrive in cool, damp conditions.

I-Spy for 20

Blackcurrants

Birds and frost are the main enemies of blackcurrants, so you may well see bushes draped with sacking or netting. Fruits appear in July and August.

I-Spy for 15

Double for either a red or white variety of currant

Strawberries

Not surprisingly, strawberries are the most popular soft fruit in Britain, yet the season is very short – from mid-May to July. Alpine strawberries produce tiny berries so at least twenty to thirty plants are needed for a good crop.

I-Spy for 10

Apples

There are hundreds of varieties of apple to choose from each autumn, but Cox's Orange Pippin is regarded by many as the best of all eaters. Its golden skin, with patches of russet brown, is distinctive.

I-Spy 10 for each of 5 different varieties

Lemon

Citrus fruits, including this 'Meyers Lemon', can be grown in Britain. They prefer a sunny aspect and need protection from the wind. This example was grown in a greenhouse.

I-Spy for 50

Figs

One of the oldest fruits known to humankind, figs are easy to cultivate but difficult to crop, and not found in many gardens. They can be grown in pots, in greenhouses, or outdoors and brought inside when frosts are likely.

I-Spy for **50**

Grapes

Grapes can be grown outdoors or in a greenhouse, and a mature grapevine will give enough fruit to make wine. The vine will last for about forty years, though no fruit will be produced for the first three. The season runs from September to October.

I-Spy for **25**

Melons

Decades ago, melons were grown in heated greenhouses on large estates. Now they are much more widely available, and are produced under cloches, inside a cold frame, or in a greenhouse. The season ranges from late July to the beginning of September.

I-Spy for **50**

Blackfly

Aphids, such as blackfly (which have damaged this viburnum stem) and greenfly, can be a serious pest. From their attacks (they feed on the plants' sap), leaves become discoloured and blistered, shoots are distorted, and the insects secrete a sticky substance – often called honey dew – on to the plant.

I-Spy for 20

Powdery mildew

Roses, vegetables, and trees are all susceptible to this fungal growth, which usually appears white and powdery. As a result, leaves turn yellow and fall, and flowers and fruits are damaged.

I-Spy for 25

45

Vine weevil
This grey-black beetle, with a short snout and antennae, feeds at night and hides in the daytime. It attacks the leaves of rhododendrons, camellias, clematis, azalea, grape vines, and strawberries.
I-Spy for 50

Garden chafer
This insect (up to 1.5 centimetres long) and the cockchafer (up to 3 centimetres long) feed on the leaves of shrubs and trees in May and June. Their grubs, which live in the soil, can eat the roots of flowers, shrubs, and vegetables.
I-Spy for 25

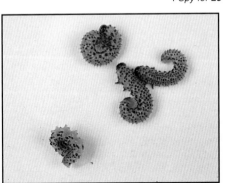

Sawflies
Conifers, willows, roses, and currants are particularly damaged by larvae of the sawfly species. They are caterpillar-like in appearance and up to 3 centimetres long.
I-Spy for 25

Rust

Fungi, known as rusts, affect a variety of shrubs, trees, indoor plants, and bulbs. Here, geranium leaves are damaged by orange and dark brown spores which are spread by rain and wind currents.

I-Spy for 20

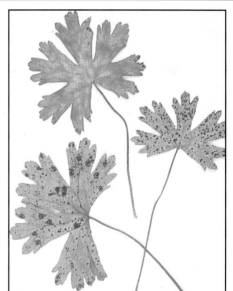

Brown rot

Apples, plums, peaches, and other fruits are prone to brown rot, a fungus that results in soft brown areas developing on the skin and penetrating to the flesh. Eventually, damaged fruit falls off the tree or becomes dry and wizened.

I-Spy for 20

INDEX

ISBN (paperback) 1 85671 153 6

Michelin Tyre Public Limited Company
Edward Hyde Building, 38 Clarendon Road, Watford, Herts WD1 1SX

MICHELIN and the Michelin Man are Registered Trademarks of Michelin

A CIP record for this title is available from the British Library.

Edited by Neil Curtis. Designed by Richard Garratt.

The Publisher gratefully acknowledges the contribution of *Practical Gardening* magazine who provided the majority of the photographs in this book, and Ian Cushway and Nicola Williams of *Practical Gardening* who selected the photographs and wrote the text. Additional photographs by *Garden News* and *Garden Answers*.

Colour reproduction by Anglia Colour.

Printed by Graficromo SA, Spain.